STEFAN GROSSMAN's
EARLY MASTERS of AMERICAN BLUES GUITAR

ANTHOLOGY OF COUNTRY BLUES GUITAR

Edited and Transcribed by STEFAN GROSSMAN

Contents

Mississippi John Hurt photos courtesy of The Sing Out Resource Center, Bethlehem, PA.
Rev. Gary Davis photos courtesy of Stefan Grossman.
Blind Boy Fuller and Lonnie Johnson photos courtesy of Yazoo Records.

Alfred Publishing Co., Inc.
16320 Roscoe Blvd., Suite 100
P.O. Box 10003
Van Nuys, CA 91410-0003
alfred.com

ISBN-10: 0-7390-4328-5 (Book & CD)
ISBN-13: 978-0-7390-4328-8 (Book & CD)

Lonnie Johnson, Mississippi John Hurt, Rev. Gary Davis and Blind Boy Fuller.
Photos courtesy of Stefan Grossman.

MASTERS OF COUNTRY BLUES GUITAR
FEATURING MISSISSIPPI JOHN HURT, REV. GARY DAVIS, BLIND BOY FULLER & LONNIE JOHNSON

by Stefan Grossman

It has been a long time! In the late 1960s, I put together a five-volume series titled *Anthology of Blues Guitar*. These books helped to define and describe various country blues styles and techniques. But there were so many more great blues arrangements still to be transcribed and understood. Finally, after many years, and a glorious summer in Spoleto, Italy, I found the time to tackle these arrangements that had been haunting me for years. The word "haunting" is quite correct. For a long time I had wanted to transcribe the guitar playing of Lonnie Johnson and the "holy blues" of Rev. Davis. The songs of Mississippi John Hurt were there to be played and studied, but I had only tickled the surface in the past. Blind Boy Fuller's vast repertoire held intriguing licks and secrets that I had put on my proverbial fingerpicker's back-burner for too long.

It could have been the rolling hills of Umbria, or the 12th century "Tower of Oil" that I was living in, or the delicious Italian "gelato" that finally inspired me to finally come to terms with a vast amount of material that had always been on my agenda. But I think the reason for my delving into this material was deeper. I had needed 25 years of blues playing, transcribing and listening to do justice to this music. It would have been impossible to transcribe Lonnie Johnson's "Stompin' 'Em Along Slow" in the 1960s. I just didn't have the ears or chops to hear all of his intricacies.

My approach to this new round of transcribing was different. In my early transcriptions, I would be satisfied with putting down a verse and a chorus. But country blues guitar was and should be today, a vibrant and improvised format. This translates into a host of variations in certain arrangements. I studied and examined each new challenge and then decided which verses and choruses would be to be transcribed. In the case of Lonnie Johnson's playing, the complete arrangements from first note to last are carefully written down. With the playing of Blind Boy Fuller, Mississippi John Hurt, and Rev. Davis, I decided to illustrate as many variations as possible within a tune. Some tunes needed only a verse and chorus while others needed several.

The result is this new series titled *Early Masters of Country Blues Guitar*. This first volume presents four of the finest players in the genre: Mississippi John Hurt, Rev. Gary Davis, Blind Boy Fuller, and Lonnie Johnson. This collection will help you "taste" country blues guitar and the vast contrasts that exist within this language. The individual studies will focus on one musician and help you better delve into their music in depth and detail. The first two books are devoted to the music of Rev. Gary Davis and Mississippi John Hurt. All in all, a lot of hot transcriptions will be rolling off the Alfred presses.

Included with each volume in this series is a CD featuring all the tunes played by the original artists. It is essential and fundamental for you to hear and absorb the original performances. These range from rare recordings from the 1920s to studio performances done in "hi-fi" in the 1960s. The combination of book and CD should be very rewarding. I have tried to clearly illustrate what sections I have transcribed. Once you have mastered these, you should be able to easily put the complete tune together.

Country blues guitar is a wonderful adventure. It has intrigued and challenged my ears and fingers for over 25 years. As I write this, I am getting ready to return to Spoleto, Italy for another July of good food, sightseeing, and best of all transcribing the music of legendary country bluesmen.

You can write to me c/o Stefan Grossman's Guitar Workshop, P.O. Box 802, Sparta, NJ 07871, if you have any question, suggestions or your own transcriptions of blues performances.

EXPLANATION OF THE TAB/MUSIC SYSTEM

"…Learning from listening is unquestionably the best way, the only way that suits this kind of music. You are setting the notes down for a record of what happened, a record that can be studied, preserved and so on, a necessary and useful companion to the recordings of the actual sounds. I keep thinking of this as I transcribe; if you could do it, it would be good to have a legend across each page reading: 'Listen to the record if you want to learn the song.'"

—Hally Wood (taken from the Publisher's Foreword to the *New Lost City Ramblers Songbook*.)

These words are most suitable for introducing the tablature system, for tablature is just a guide and should be used in conjunction with the recordings. Tablature is not like music notation, however the combination of TAB and music in an arrangement forms a complete language. Used together with the original recordings, they give a total picture of the music.

The TAB system does not attempt to show rhythms or accents. These can be found on the music or heard in the recordings. Music notation tackles these articulations to a degree, but the overall sensations, the feel and the soul of music cannot be wholly captured on the written page. In the words of the great Sufi Hazrat Inayat Khan, "…the traditional ancient songs of India composed by great Masters have been handed down from father to son. The way music is taught is different from the Western way. It is not always written, but is taught by imitation. The teacher sings and the pupil imitates and the intricacies and subtleties are learned by imitation."

This is the theme I've tried to interpolate into the tablature. Tablature is the roadmap and you are the driver. Now to the TAB.

Each space indicates a string. The top space represents the first string, second space the second string, etc. A zero means an open string, a number in the space indicates the fretted position, for instance a 1 in a space indicates the first fret of that string.

In the diagram below, the zero is on the second string and indicates the open second string is played. The 1 is placed on the third string and signifies the first fret of the third string. Likewise, the 4 is in the fourth space and indicates the fourth fret of the fourth string.

Generally, for fingerpicking styles you will be playing the thumb, index, and middle fingers of your picking hand. To indicate the picking finger in TAB, the stems go up and line up down from the numbers.

A. A stem down means that your thumb strikes the note.

B. If a stem is up, your index or middle finger strikes the note. The choice of finger is left up to you, as your fingers will dictate what is most comfortable, especially when playing a song up to tempo!

C. The diagram below shows an open sixth string played with the thumb followed by the second fret of the third string played with the index or middle finger:

In most cases, the thumb will play an alternating bass pattern, usually on the bass strings. The index and middle fingers play melodic notes on the first, second and third strings. Please remember, this is not a rule; there are many exceptions.

In fingerpicking there are two "picking" styles: regular picking and "pinching" two notes together. A pinch is shown in the TAB by a line connecting two notes. A variation of this can also be two treble notes pinched with a bass note. Follow the examples below from left to right.

1) The open sixth string is played with the thumb.

2) The first fret of the sixth string is pinched together with the third fret on the third string. The sixth string is played with the thumb, the third string with the index finger.

3) The thumb strikes the third fret of the fourth string.

4) The first fret/sixth string is played with the thumb; it's pinched with two notes in the treble. The index and middle fingers strike the first fret/first string and the third fret/second string.

5) The next note is the index finger hitting the first fret/second string.

6) Lastly, the bass note is played with the thumb on the third fret/fourth string.

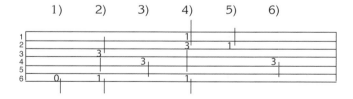

There are certain places in blues and contemporary guitar that call for the use of either strumming techniques or accented bass notes. The TAB illustrates these as follows:

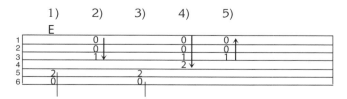

1) The thumb hits the open sixth string and the second fret on the fifth string should also sound. For example, play an E chord. Now strike the open string and vary the force of your attack. Try hitting it hard enough so that the fifth string vibrates as well. This technique is very important for developing a full sound and the right alternating bass sound.

2) Next, the arrow notation indicates a brush and the arrowhead indicates the direction of the brush.

   A. If the arrowhead is pointed down, the hand brushes up towards the sixth string.

   B. If pointed up, the hand brushes down towards the first string.

   C. The number of strings to be played by the brush is shown by the length of the arrows. For example, this arrow shows a brush up toward the sixth string, but indicates to strike only the first, second and third strings.

   D. The brush can be done with your whole hand, index finger or middle and ring finger. Let comfort plus a full and "right" sound guide your choice.

3) The third set of notes again shows the sixth string/open bass note played with the thumb and being struck hard enough to make the fifth string/second fretted position sound.

4) Once more, an arrow pointed downward indicates a brush up. This example forms an E chord and the brush up includes the first, second, third, and fourth strings.

5) The last set of notes has an arrow pointed upward, indicating a brush downward striking the first, second, and third strings.

Here are several special effects that are also symbolized in tablature:

1) HAMMER-ON: Designated by an "H" which is placed after the stem on the fret to be hammered. In the example above, fret the second fret/fifth string and pick it with your thumb. Then "hammer-on" (hit hard) the third fret/fifth string (i.e., fret the third fret/fifth string). This is an all-in-one, continuous motion which will produce two notes rapidly with one picking finger strike.

2) WHAM: Designated by a "W." In the example the eighth fret/second string is "whammed" and played with the seventh fret/first string. Both notes are played together with your index and middle fingers respectively. The whammed note is "stretched." We do this by literally bending the note up. We can "wham" the note up a half tone, full tone, etc.

3) HARMONICS: Symbolized by a dot (•). To play a harmonic, gently lay your finger directly above the indicated fret (don't press down!) The two notes in the example are both harmonics. The first on the twelfth fret/third string is played with the index/middle finger, while the second note—twelfth fret/fourth string—is played with the thumb.

4) SLIDE: Shown with a dash (–). Play the second fret/sixth string and then slide up to the fourth fret of the sixth string. This is a continuous movement, the string is struck once with your thumb.

5) PULL-OFF: "P" designates a "pull-off." Fret both the seventh and ninth frets on the second string. Play the ninth fret with your index/middle finger and then quickly remove it in the same stroke, leaving the seventh fret/second string. Pull-offs are generally in a downward direction.

6) In certain cases, other specific symbols are added to the TAB:

   A. For ARTIFICIAL HARMONICS, an "X" is placed after the fretted position.

   B. For SNAPPING, a note an indication may be given with a symbol or the written word.

Many times, these special techniques are combined. For instance, putting a pull-off and a hammer-on together. Coordination of your fretting and picking hands will be complex initially, but the end results are exciting and fun to play.

PICKING HAND POSITION FOR FINGERPICKING STYLES

The Classical and Flamenco schools have strict right-hand rules, however for this style of acoustic fingerpicking, there are no rules, only suggestions. Your right hand position should be dictated by comfort, however in observation of many well-known fingerpickers, I found one hand position similarity—they all tend to rest their little finger and/or ring finger on the face of the guitar. This seems to help their balance for accenting notes and control of the guitar. Experiment with this position, it may feel uncomfortable at first. I ask my students to perfect this position and then compare the sound to when their finger(s) were not placed on the face of the guitar. They usually find the sound is greatly improved when some contact is kept with the guitar face.

MUSIC NOTATION

We have somewhat adapted the music notation in that this also shows whether the note is picked with your thumb or index/middle fingers. The stems of the music notes correspond to the direction of the TAB stems. I hope this will make the music notation clearer to fingerpicking guitarists.

I hope you will feel at home and comfortable with the tablature and musical notations. Remember, these are only road maps indicating where and how you should place your fingers. The playing and musical interpretation is up to you.

Mississippi John Hurt

To listen to a complete collection of John Hurt's original recordings is to visit an America that no longer exists and can only be imperfectly imagined. It is to fly backwards a full fifty years not to a recording studio, but to the hill country town of Avalon, Mississippi, which had no significance beyond its own minuscule boundaries. Fewer than a hundred persons lived there in the 1920s, and most of the outsiders who were familiar with it as a place name would have known Avalon merely as the third rail stop going north of Greenwood, towards Grenada. There for most of his life, Hurt worked as a farm hand and played guitar in his spare time for the amusement of neighbors whose existence was otherwise much like his own. Socially, his music was the local equivalent of a radio, a phonograph, or the as yet uninvented television, existing as a familiar amusement to fill empty time in a pleasant fashion. An Avalonian who enjoyed Hurt would probably be no more likely to mull over his music than consider the ingredients of the local corn whiskey Hurt's brother manufactured.

Though few outsiders would now prefer such whiskey to today's bona fide brands, Hurt's equally provincial music has endured in a fashion its unprepossessing creator could scarcely fathom. Some fifty years after he recorded, when technology has usurped his social function, his music is classified as "folk" music. If this unfortunate term means music that is remote from the pop mainstream and is the equivalent of home-brew or homespun clothing, Hurt's work qualified as such; for his entire life (which began in 1894 at Teoc and ended in 1967) his musical horizons seemed no larger than his home town. Yet the catch-all label "folk" invariably diminishes a sensible understanding of Hurt's music as it related to black music of his time and place. Between the 1900 and 1940, there were four discernible streams of accompanied non-church music performed by blacks, all of which used the same genres (blues, "rags", and pop songs) in different ways for different purposes. There was household music, street music, dance music, and music performed by an amateur with no interest in financial gain, unencumbered by the obvious ulterior motives that entered into the calculations of opportunistic blues singers. His was music with no conventional non-musical gimmicks appended, such as a tearjerker tale designed to coax hand-outs from passersby or to whitewash the negative social image of blues singers (by making them seem pitiable rather than predatory, as they were otherwise viewed), or the sexual overtures (surreptitious or overt) that blues singers routinely injected into what was supposedly a medium of entertainment.

Perhaps it was for this reason that Hurt had none of the religious conflicts so characteristic of his contemporaries; his playing was not an assumption of a social role, or a bid for approval that made him the inherent competitor of the local preacher.

Though Hurt recalled playing for local parties, his inability to recall specific dances that accompanied his songs clearly indicates that his was not performance music, except on a square dance level. His is decidedly not a music designed or arranged for public presentation, but music others might listen to while relaxing in Hurt's company. The household character of his playing is discernible in his soft picking touch, which makes him project less than a dance guitarist like Blind Blake or Charlie Patton. It is also discernible in his lack of vocal projection; the singer does nothing to amplify the ordinary volume by using dynamics. Indeed, Hurt's soft voice would have precluded his ever considering a musical career, and it was probably because of it that he always refused to regard himself as a blues singer.

Paradoxically, his lack of professionalism served to make his guitar-playing more intricate than that of most blues singers. It freed him from the necessity of thinking in terms of dance tempos and thus playing slowly enough to emphasize the gymnastic character of his accents. He could play with as much speed or subtlety as he was capable of attaining through his fingers alone. Moreover, he could approach his instrument in a way that makes more sense to modern ears than it would have to a black audience of his age—as an accompanying instrument. Most blues guitarists, by contrast, used no picking pattern, because their voices served as rhythm instruments. Their over-riding goal was to correlate vocal and guitar accenting; such a correspondence cannot be achieved if one uses an inflexible pick pattern, unless one's lyrics all scan identically. Hurt's development of a strict picking pattern (a self-taught one, he maintained) was foreign to black musicianship and had no real counterpart, save Elizabeth Cotton. His radically unorthodox approach was probably attributable to his lack of vocal prowess; unlike Charlie Patton, he did not think as a vocalist while playing guitar. Among Mississippians, his closest counterpart in this respect was Bo Carter (Yazoo 1014, 1034 and 1064) who, like Hurt, used a blues format but never worked as a blues singer.

Hurt's music also harks back to an age when black music must have had a predominately amateurish cast. He began playing in 1903—a time when guitars were relatively rare. His mature repertoire had only superficial reference to the Mississippi blues W.C. Handy first heard around the same year. When Hurt first performed at parties around 1906 or 1907, he recalled, "I sing songs like 'Hop Join' (a variant of 'Frankie and Johnnie') an' 'Good Morning Miss Carrie'…" Neither of these were blues. Until around 1916, when he worked as a track liner for some five months, he was a farmer with no occasion to travel. As a rail hand, he learned an a cappella rendition of "Spike Driver" from a "caller" named Walter Jackson, who sang airs while co-workers supplied rhythmic or choral effects. A cousin taught him the already dated "Casey Jones" in the same period.

Around 1923, Hurt first teamed up with the local white fiddler Willie Narmour, who used him as a square dance guitarist when his usual accompanist, Shell Smith, could not make an engagement. On these occasions, Hurt functioned as a flatpicker. When an Okeh scout visited Avalon some four years later to make recording arrangements for Narmour and Smith (who had garnished their contract by winning a fiddle contest) and inquired about other musicians, Hurt was recommended to him. A brief audition (of one and a half songs) enabled Hurt to record in Memphis the following February. Only two of his eight sides were issued. A New York session that December resulted in five records. His records had some appeal to whites, and his success might have been greater had his apparently racist sponsors seen fit to feature him in the label's "white" catalogue. How indifferent Hurt was to success as a blues singer is illustrated by the fact that he met Lonnie Johnson in New York, but cribbed nothing from the blues' premier commercial attraction.

Man" or "Frankie" that he sounds most exciting.

"Frankie" is one of Hurt's few accomplishments in which texture seems paramount. Its most prominent filler riff is more evocative of B.F. Shelton's accenting than that of a blues guitarist. It contains his most spectacular thumbing, and attains a remarkable fullness of sound that is somewhat akin to the less disciplined or regular picking of Charlie Patton's "Bo Weavil" (Yazoo 1020), which may likewise be in "Spanish" tuning. Whereas Patton achieves his effects on open strings, Hurt's tune is melodically ambitious and more demanding. Because he uses a pattern pick, however, the correlation between his vocal and guitar melody notes is imprecise, and the work succeeds best when played instrumentally. It nevertheless remains the best version of an insipid ditty that few guitarists (including Patton) treated successfully, perhaps owing to its unorthodox phrasing.

Unlike his blues counterparts, Hurt had no recognizable signature song. From a guitar stand-point, his chief accomplishment was his ability to attain a flowing effect in "rag" ditties that were typically played in a jerky fashion by artists (like Furry Lewis or Sam Collins) who were unable to integrate an alternating bass with an irregularly accented melodic line. Both "Stack O' Lee" and "Ain't No Tellin' (a Pallet On the Floor)" have an unusually steady pulse that attests to Hurt's superior thumb work. At the same time, Hurt's preoccupation with rhythmic smoothness tends to restrict melodic expressiveness and result in bland-sounding guitar textures, as his picking pattern is best facilitated by primary chord positions (whose pitch most closely corresponds to that of open E, A, and D strings).

Because he tends to impose his pick pattern on whatever material he plays, the sound of blues like "Avalon" or "Big Leg Blues" doesn't differ notably from that of "rag" songs like "Stack O' Lee." It is when Hurt discards his patented approach on works like "Candy

"Ain't No Tellin'" belongs to the "rag song" genre and utilizes C shapes. Only the last tune (an eight-bar song that uses the final bar as an instrumental fill) is played according to a fixed phrasing pattern, a sure sign of white influence. "Avalon" is an unconventional blues played with E shapes: a short (five beat) vocal phrase is typically followed by two one-measure tonic riffs, which give the song a quasi-instrumental flavor. "Big Leg Blues" also features a truncated vocal phrase, possibly indicating an artist who regards vocalizing as a duty rather than an opportunity to impress listeners. When Hurt departs from his fixed thumb pattern at the end of each break to play fingered bass notes, his lack of picking flexibility translates into awkwardness.

—From the sleeve notes of *Mississippi John Hurt –1926 Sessions Yazoo Records 1065*. Used with kind permission.

Big Leg Blues

By
John Hurt

Raise up, Baby, get your big leg off - a' mine;

Raise up, Ba-by, get your big leg off-a'mine __ ; They're so

heav-y, make a good man change his mind.

Raise up, baby, get your big leg offa mine,
Raise up, baby, get your big leg offa mine,
They're so heavy, make a good man change his mind.

I asked you, baby, to come and hold my head,
I asked you, baby, to come and hold my head,
Send me word that you'd rather see me dead.

I'm goin', I'm goin', your cryin' won't make me stay,
I'm goin', I'm goin', cryin' won't make me stay,
More you cry, the further you drive me away.

Some crave high yellow, I like black and brown,
Some crave high yellow, I like black and brown,
Black won't quit you, brown won't lay you down.

It was late at midnight and the moon shine bright like day,
It was late at midnight and moon shines bright like day,
I seen your faror* goin' up the right of way.

*The spelling of "faror," a Mississippi blues synonym for girlfriend, is problematic. It is pronounced like "pharaoh." The late Johnnie Temple provided blues researcher Gayle Wardlow with the spelling used.

Big Leg Blues

By
John Hurt

11

Stack O' Lee Blues

By
John Hurt

Police Officer, how can it be?
You can 'rest everybody but cruel Stack O' Lee.
That bad man, oh, cruel Stack O' Lee.

Billy de Lyon told Stack O' Lee, "Please don't take my life.
I got two little babies, and a darlin' lovin' wife."
That bad man, oh, cruel Stack O' Lee.

"What I care about your little babies, your darlin' lovin' wife?
You done stole my Stetson hat, I'm bound to take your life."
That bad man, cruel Stack O' Lee.

Fourth and fifth verses hummed.

...with the forty-four.
When I spied Billy de Lyon, he was lyin' down on the floor.
That bad man, oh cruel Stack O' Lee.

"Gentlemans of the jury, what do you think of that?
Stack O' Lee killed Billy de Lyon about a five-dollar Stetson hat."
That bad man, oh, cruel Stack O' Lee.

And all they gathered, hands way up high,
At twelve o'clock they killed him, they's all glad to see him die.
That bad man, oh, cruel Stack O' Lee.

Stack O' Lee Blues

By
John Hurt

Ain't No Tellin'

By
John Hurt

Don't let my good girl catch you here

Don't let my good girl catch you here   She

might shoot you - May cut and stob you too

Ain't no tel-lin' what she might do!

Don't you let my good girl catch you here.
Don't you let my good girl catch you here.
She might shoot you, may cut ya and starve you too.
Ain't no tellin, what, she might do.

I'm up the country where the col' sleet and snow.
I'm up the country where the col' sleet and snow.
Ain't no telling how much further I may go.

Eatin' my breakfast here, my dinner in Tennessee.
Eatin' my breakfast here, my dinner in Tennessee.
I tol' you I was comin', baby, won't you look for me.
Hey, hey, such lookin' the class.

The way I'm sleepin' my back and shoulders tired.
Way I'm sleepin' babe, my back and shoulders tired.
Gonna turn over, try it on the side.

Don't you let, my good girl catch you here.
She, might shoot you, may cut you and starve you too.
Ain't no tellin', what, she might do.

Ain't No Tellin'

By
John Hurt

FIRST GUITAR BREAK

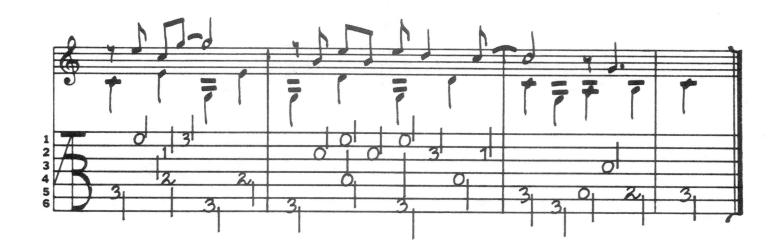

Frankie

By
John Hurt

Frank-ie was a good girl Ev-'ry-bod-y know; She paid one-hun-dred dol-lars For Al-bert's suit of clothes He's her man But he did her wrong

Frankie was a good girl, everybody know,
She paid 100 dollars for Albert's suit of clothes.
He's her man, but he did her wrong.

Frankie went down to the corner saloon,
    she ordered her a glass of beer,
She asked the barkeeper, "Has my lovin' Albert
    been here?"
"He's been here, but he's gone again."

"Ain't gonna tell you no story, Frankie, I ain't
    gonna tell you no lie."
Says, "Albert a-passed about a hour ago, with a
    girl you call Alice Frye.
He's your man, and he's doin' me wrong."

Frankie went down to the corner saloon,
    she didn't go to be gone long,
She peeked through keyhole in the door,
    spied Albert in Alice's arm.
He's my man, and he's doin' me wrong."

Frankie called Albert, Albert says, "I don't hear."
"If you don't come to the woman you love,
    gonna haul you outta here.

He's my man, and you's doin' me wrong."

Frankie shot old Albert, she shot him 3 or 4 times.
Says, "Stand back, I'm smokin' my gun, let me see
    is Albert dyin'.
He's my man, and he did me wrong."

Frankie and the judge walked outta the stand,
    and walked out side by side.
The judge says, "Frankie, you're gonna be justified.
Killin' a man, and he did you wrong."

Frankie was a good girl, everybody know,
She paid 100 dollars for Albert's suit of clothes.
He's her man, and he did her wrong.

Said, "Turn me over, mother, turn me over slow,
It may be my last time, you won't turn me no
    more.
He's my ..."

Says, Frankie was a good girl, everybody know,
She paid 100 dollars for Albert's suit of clothes.
He's her man, and he did her wrong.

Frankie

By
John Hurt

REV. GARY DAVIS

Gary Davis was born in 1896 in Lawrence County, South Carolina. He was brought up in the country by his elderly grandmother. He was left blind at an early age and recalls that his loss of sight occurred after a doctor put "some drops" into his eyes. His grandmother made him his first guitar and by his early teens he was and accomplished musician on the five-string banjo, harmonica, and guitar. He played in a string band in Greenville, South Carolina and there met Willie Walker (cf Yazoo L-1013, East Coast Blues) whose many ragtime instrumentals Reverend Davis can play. In 1933, he was ordained as a minister. During the thirties, he traveled and lived in Durham, North Carolina and attended a school for the blind in that city. It was in Durham that he met and played with Blind Boy Fuller, Bull City Red, and Sonny Terry.

Reverend Davis has always had a great admiration for the playing of Lonnie Johnson, Buddy Moss, Willie Walker, and Blind Blake, but he never thought to imitate. Instead he concentrated on developing his own style. It was this "style" that he taught to Blind Boy Fuller, Bull City Red, and Brownie McGhee and that the majority of blues listeners tend to classify as Fuller's (Fuller came to Davis with only the knowledge of playing in open tunings and with a bottleneck.) After their association, Fuller recorded many of the pieces that Davis had taught him. It is apparent on hearing Fuller's recordings of "Twelve Gates," "Piccolo Rag," "She's Funny That Way," "Mama," and "Let Me Lay It On You" that these were second-hand imitations taken from another source. I have verified this teacher/student relationship over the past ten years by taping Reverend Davis doing one song in many different styles and then in the way he showed it to Fuller.

Fuller, Davis, and Bull City Red traveled to New York in July of 1935 to record. This was to be the first in a long series of successful recordings for Fuller, but for Reverend Davis it was a short lived experience. He recorded 15 songs under the name Blind Gary and accompanied several of Fuller's tunes playing second guitar. Davis was very dissatisfied with his personal treatment and payment and this—coupled with the A & R man's insistence to record blues when Davis had only desired to record gospel numbers—ended up in an argument. The result was that the company never recorded "Blind Gary" again.

Davis them moved up to New York City in the forties and has lived there ever since. He recorded a rare 78 in 1949 and was further recorded once the "folk revival" got under way. During the fifties and sixties, he was a favorite on the concert and club circuits where the emphasis for this new "white" audience was on guitar techniques. In the last fifteen years he has recorded nine LP's which demonstrate his skill for guitar instrumentals, gospel singing, and carnival show songs.

Blues historians tend to classify the guitar style of Reverend Davis as an imitation of Blind Blake's, but this is quite absurd. Blake's technique was limited to his style of music. Davis uses a much more complicated approach to guitar playing which employs rhythmic and linear counterpoint behind a sung musical statement. His instrumentals go beyond the ordinary "dance rag" and can depict a marching band, a battle, a broken car, or the dreams of the devil. Reverend Davis has also perfected more than one style. He can play in the gentle manner of John Hurt ("You Got the Pocket Book I Got the Key," "Cocaine Blues," "Candyman") or the more primitive bottleneck style ("Whistlin' Blues") or even double thumb frail banjo dance tunes ("Cripple Creek") or play carnival style banjo ("Come Down and See Me Sometime"). But his major achievement is developing a guitar style that incorporated more than a syncopated bass or an alternating bass but used a variation of these played against a treble melody that was coupled with a middle registered harmony. It is this style that is clearly shown on this tape. During his youth, Davis broke his left hand wrist and it set in an unusual position. This allowed him to play many unorthodox chord positions. His right-hand picking technique is based on the use of two fingers, thumb and index. There are no rules for the manner in which these two are used. Many times, the thumb plays treble notes to give them the right accent. However, when playing single-string runs, he generally alternates every other note between thumb and index. This produces a very "accented" rhythmic quality. He has developed "rolls" that double-time the rhythm or accentuate the existing time signature. These are achieved by allowing the thumb to play a roll against the index finger playing the dominant note in that key. He uses a thumb pick for some songs and prefers to play without picks for the softer carnival show tunes.

It is hard for me to tell when Reverend Davis's style matured. The 1935 recordings have a rough vocal quality about them but a very competent guitar sound. This could be attributed to his youth, the bad atmosphere in the studio created by the situation, or Davis's not using the capo in the proper position on the guitar.

The later recordings done in 1949 show a much more controlled sound. The guitar used on his 1935 session was a steel bodied National Resonator guitar. This was ideal for street-singing as it could project a powerful tone, but for recordings it had many disadvantages. This model of guitar tends to exaggerate the treble note and diminish the clarity of the bass strings. On the 1949 sides, he is using a wooden bodied Gibson guitar that is more suitable for his playing. This could account for the difference in atmosphere besides the difference in recording techniques.

Davis's singing technique depends on the type of material he is doing. For religious pieces, he tends to preach, shout and sing with as much intensity as possible. His blues are marked by interesting guitar arrangements against an almost spoken verse. His carnival show songs tend to have softer guitar arrangements that are used solely as an accompaniment and where his singing is more melodic but never with the intensity of his gospel music.

—From the sleeve note of *Reverend Gary Davis —1935-1949*
Yazoo Records 1023. Used with kind permission.

Hesitation Blues

Trad. Arr. by
Rev. Gary Davis

I woke up this morn-in' just 'bout half past four,

He-si-ta-tion Blues was knock-ing on my door; Tell me,

how long do I, Ba-by, have to wait?

Can I get you now – Why must I he-si-tate?

HESITATION BLUES

Trad. Arr. by
Rev. Gary Davis

I woke up this morning just 'bout half past four
Hesitation blues was knocking on my door

Refrain:
Tell me, how long, do I baby, have to wait
Can I let you know? Why must I hesitate?

Ain't no use in me working so hard
I got me two good women
working in the rich folks' yard

I ain't your good man,
ain't your good man's son
But I can get in the place of your good man,
'til your good man comes

Well, I ain't no miller,
ain't no miller's son
But I can grind a little corn,
'til the miller comes

I ain't no wine presser,
ain't no wine presser's son
But I can buy you a little groceries,
'til the grocery man comes

I ain't no cradle rocker,
ain't no cradle rocker's son
But I can do a little rockin' for you,
'til the rocker man comes

Well, I ain't no doctor,
ain't no doctor's son
But I can cure a few cases,
'til the doctor comes

Eagle on the dollar say, "In God We Trust"
Woman flashy, wants a man but I declare
she want a dollar first

I ain't no bookkeeper,
ain't no bookkeeper's son
But I can keep a few books,
'til the bookkeeper comes

I ain't no milkman,
ain't no milkman's son
But I can keep you supplied,
'til your milkman comes

I ain't no chauffeur,
ain't no chauffeur's son
But I can do a little driving,
'til your chauffeur comes

Well, I ain't no back-breaker,
ain't no back-breaker's son
But I can stretch out my back,
'til your back-breaker comes

I ain't got no woman and I ain't got no kid
Ain't got no daughter to be bothered with

I ain't no rent payer,
ain't no rent payer's son
But I can scrape up a few rents,
'til the rent payer comes

Well, I ain't been to heaven but I've been told
St. Peter learnt the angels how to do the Jelly Roll

Me and my buddy and two or three more
We get good women everywhere we go

Well, I hitched up the mule
and the mule wouldn't pull
Took the hunches off the mule
and put the hunches on the bull

Blacker the berry the sweeter the juice
I'd be a fool if I quit the woman I got
because it ain't no use

I got hesitating stockings,
hesitating shoes
I got a hesitating woman
singing me the hesitating blues

My good gal quit me,
I ain't going to wear no black
I always got something to make her
come running back

Men in the country hollering, "Whoa, haw, gee!"*
Women in the city flying around
asking the question, "Who wants me?"

Ashes to ashes and dust to dust
Just show me a woman that a man can trust

You know, my mother told me
when I was just six years old
I'm going to be a good women getter,
God bless your soul

*Whoa, haw, gee means: "Stop, go toward the left,
 go toward the right.

Hesitation Blues

Trad. Arr. by
Rev. Gary Davis

FIRST GUITAR BREAK

THIRD GUITAR BREAK

27

Soldier's Drill

Music by
Rev. Gary Davis

"KEY OF F" SECTION

SEE VARIATIONS

TO "KEY OF C" SECTION

"F" SECTION ENDING VARIATION

KEY OF "C" SECTION

VARIATION SECTION

I'm Throwing Up My Hands

By
Rev. Gary Davis

There is one thing, sure do worry me. *(2x)*
My good gal packed her suitcase, walked off and left poor me.

Lord, Lord, see what a fix she left me in. *(2x)*
I ain't got no home, and ain't got no friends.

I'm going away to wear you off my mind. *(2x)*
Said I won't be here wringing my hands and crying.

I'm Throwing Up My Hands

By
Rev. Gary Davis

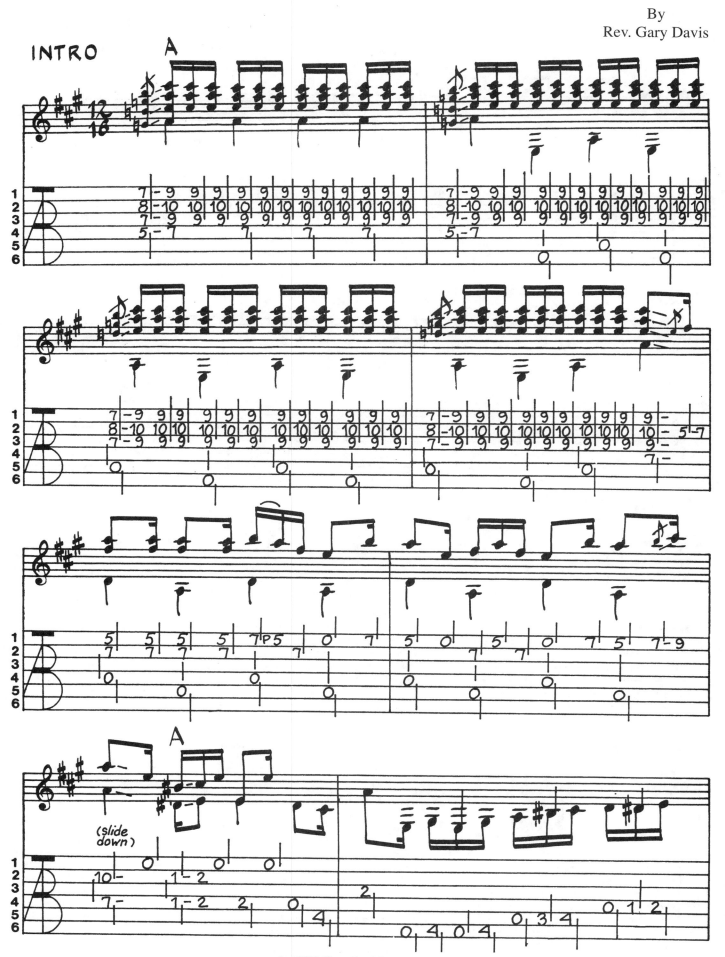

FOURTH VERSE

SECOND GUITAR BREAK

THIRD GUITAR BREAK

Baby, Let Me Lay It On You

Trad. Arr. by
Rev. Gary Davis

Baby, let me lay it on you. Baby, let me lay it on you.
I'd give your everything in this God almighty world, if you just let me lay it on you.
Please sugar, let me lay it on you. Please m'am! let me lay it on you.
I'd give you everything in this God almighty world, if you just let me lay it on you.
Please m'am, let me lay it on you.

I'd buy you a brand new car; buy you a motorcycle on the side.
I'd give you everything in a God almighty world, just let me lay it on you, please.
Please sugar I'd buy you a Greyhound bus, and give you a nice jet plane
I'd tell you what I'll do, I'll run behind, here's $1000, let me lay it on you, any jet complaints?
let me lay it on you, cadillac and a motorcycle, let me lay it on you

BLIND BOY FULLER

One of the most popular East Coast bluesmen (along with Blind Blake and Tampa Red), Blind Boy Fuller was the last commercially successful country blues artist whose style had either a regional basis or regional impact. He became a bestseller at a time when the commercial blues market was pre-empted by slow Chicago band blues. Unlike his popular contemporaries, Kokomo Arnold (Yazoo 1049) and Bo Carter (Yazoo 1014 and 1034), who similarly echoed pre-1930s music, Fuller attracted numerous imitators, including Brownie McGhee, whose debut records billed him as "Blind Boy No. 2". Yet none of Fuller's musical relatives managed to attain his blend of lively showmanship and skillful technique, which made him a stand-out in a region that abounded with polished instrumentalists. Unlike most blues artists, Fuller can be completely engaging as both a party-oriented or "jive" performer, and a somber blues-man. In this respect, he invites comparison to Charlie Patton.

Fuller's life has been documented by Bruce Bastin in *Crying for the Carolines* (Studio Vista: 1971). He was born Fulton Allen between 1908 and 1909 in Wadesborom, the county seat of Anson County, North Carolina, located near the South Carolina border. In the mid-1920s he moved to Rockingham, a town then numbering 2,500 that was Wadesboro's nearest eastern neighbor of consequence. Around 1928, Fuller lost his last vestige of sight (the cause of his blindness remains unknown) and began playing guitar professionally. He first located his career in the state's most populous city, Winston-Salem, where he often played for tobacco workers. In the early 1930s, after a two month interlude in Danville, Virginia, he settled in Durham, North Carolina, a city over 50,000. He was to live there for the rest of his life.

According to Gary Davis (Yazoo 1023), who met him in Durham in 1935, Fuller's early repertoire was bottleneck-oriented. Some idea of what he sounded like during his formative years emerges on "Homesick and Lonesome Blues," one of Fuller's few recorded bottleneck pieces. It is played in open E tuning (with the guitar tuned a half-step low) and is basically in the style of Bumble Bee Slim's "No Women No Nickel" (Yazoo 1012), with strong suggestions on Tampa Red (Yazoo 1039), falling somewhere between the two in terms of smoothness and finesse. At the same time he contrives individual flourishes, as when he breaks into an ascending octave bass associated with versions of "Big Road Blues," but resolves it as a separate instrumental figure.

It is Davis who is credited with putting the finishing touches on Fuller, as well as teaching him a number of his later-recorded themes. It was once a tendency among blues enthusiasts to consider Fuller as basically a poor man's Davis, a comparison fostered more by the latter's recollections ("He was one of my pupils") than an actual assessment of Fuller's repertoire. Though Fuller's basic accompaniment in the A position (such as Mamie) is patterned after Davis's "I'm Throwin' Up My Hands" (Yazoo 1023), his accompaniments in the C, D ("Painful Hearted Man"), and E position show no Davis influence whatsoever. His earliest mentor, in fact was probably Tampa Red, whose "What's That Tastes Like Gravy?" of 1929 (1039) is emulated by Fuller on "Truckin' My Blues Away" (a sixteen-bar "ragtime" tune played in the C position, capoed to D). Fuller's bluesier orientation is discernible in his tendency to play dance music that remained essentially foreign to Davis, and in a more rhythmic integration of vocal and guitar than is attained by Davis (who saw instrumentation as an end in itself) on secular recordings. Fuller's bouncier beat (as well as his more accomplished singing) doubtless contributed to his relatively greater success among contemporaries.

In any event, Fuller became one of the decade's best-selling bluesmen following his discovery by the late James Baxter Long, who retailed records in a Durham department store and similarly promoted Davis, Brownie McGhee, and Sonny Terry. Between 1935 and 1940 he recorded 135 titles (including eight spirituals as "Brother George"). His position as an American Record Company mainstay can be seen through the fact that he recorded more sides for the label in that period than Big Bill (Yazoo 1035), its other leading blues attraction. Many Fuller compositions were credited to Long, who tried to arrange sessions whenever Fuller (with or without his assistance) had worked up ten themes in advance. Long felt that his customers had a decided taste for the "double-entendre" songs that were Fuller's forte, and that these songs reflected the life styles of bluesmen and their clientele, "Ninety per cent of 'em back in that day was a backdoor man." It is said that Fuller (who died in February, 1941, at the age of thirty-two) made a deathbed religious conversion, indicating that he (like many bluesmen) saw a sickness as heavenly retribution for blues-playing.

—From the sleeve notes *Blind Boy Fulller Truckin' My Blues Away* Yazoo Records 1060. Used with kind permission.

Jivin' Woman Blues

By
Blind Boy Fuller

Say you can never tell, what some of these women's mind. (2x)
Yeah, keep you huggin' and kissin' you and treatin' you all the time.

Said, I went home this morning, 'twixt nine thirty and ten. (2x)
Yeah, I met that woman's second man, right right back in my den.

Says, she's a dirty mistreater and she drove me from her door. (2x)
Yeah, the good book said mama, you got to reap just what you sow.

Said, a woman's just like a dollar, dollar go from hand to hand. (2x)
Yeah, some these low down women just run from man to man.

Now you know my woman says she loves me, she's been loving me all her life. (2x)
Yeah, she met a second man on that corner, she told him that same lie twice.

Jivin' Woman Blues

By
Blind Boy Fuller

INTRO (FIRST GUITAR BREAK)

I Crave My Pig Meat

By
Blind Boy Fuller

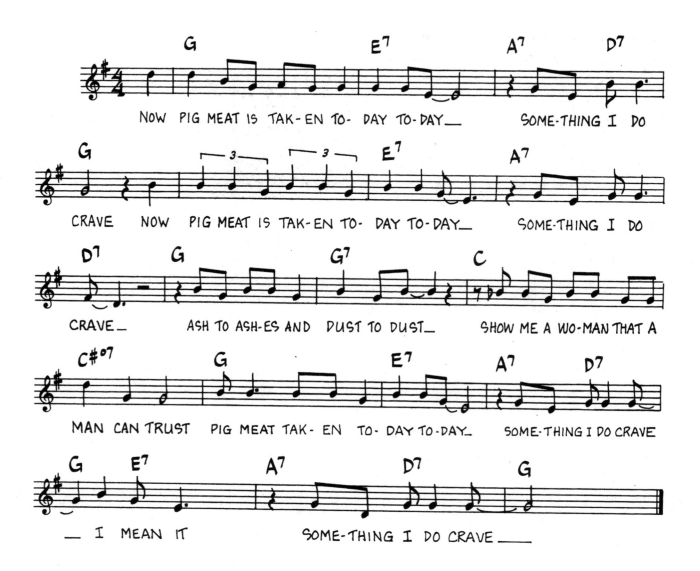

I Crave My Pig Meat

By
Blind Boy Fuller

Now pigmeat is taken today, something I do crave.
Now pigmeat is taken today, something I do crave
Ashes to ashes and dust to dust,
Show me a woman that a man can trust.
Now pigmeat is taken today today, something I do crave, I mean it, something I do crave.

Now pigmeat is kicking today today, something I do crave.
Now pigmeat is kicking today today, something I do crave
Had a little gal she was little and low,
She used to let me shake it but she won't no more.
Now pigmeat is kicking today today, something I do crave, I mean it, something I do crave.

Now pigmeat is kicking today today, something I do crave.
Now pigmeat is kicking today today, something I do crave
Looked down that road as far as I could see,
The boys had my woman and the blues had me.
Now pigmeat is kicking today today, something I do crave, I mean it, something I do crave.

Now pigmeat is kicking today today, something I do crave.
Now pigmeat is kicking today today, something I do crave
Ashes to ashes and sand to sand,
Show me a woman ain't got a backdoor man.
Now pigmeat is kicking today today, something I do crave, I mean it, something I do crave.

I Crave My Pig Meat

By
Blind Boy Fuller

SECOND GUITAR BREAK

Careless Love

By
Blind Boy Fuller

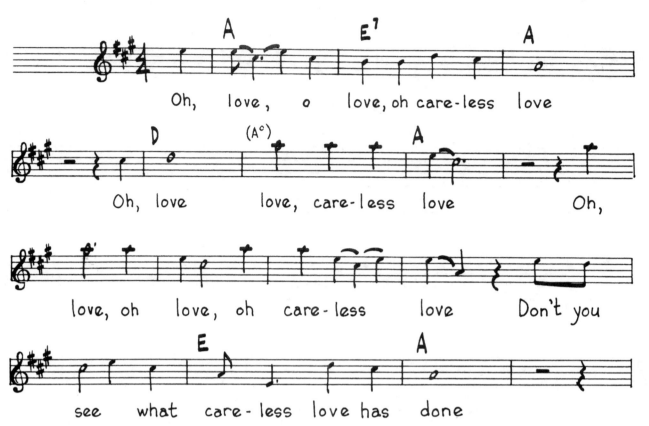

Oh, love, oh, love, careless love.
Oh, love, love, oh, careless love.
Oh, love, oh, love, oh, careless love.
Don't you see, what careless lovers do.

And it cause' you to leave your used to home.
And it cause' you to leave, cause' you to moan.
And it cause' you to leave and caused you to moan.
And it caused you have to leave your happy home.

Now love, oh, love, careless love.
Oh, love, love, oh, careless love.
And it's love, oh, love, I mean, oh, careless love.
I want you to see, what careless love has done.

Now it's Lord have mercy on poor me.
And it's Lord have mercy on poor me.
And it's Lord have mercy mmmm poor me.
It's nothin' but troublin' in the world I see.

Now all my money you could spend.
Says all, my money that you could spend.
Now it's all my money that you could spend.
Even past my door and you wouldn't look in.

Careless Love

By
Blind Boy Fuller

58

You Never Can Tell

By
Blind Boy Fuller

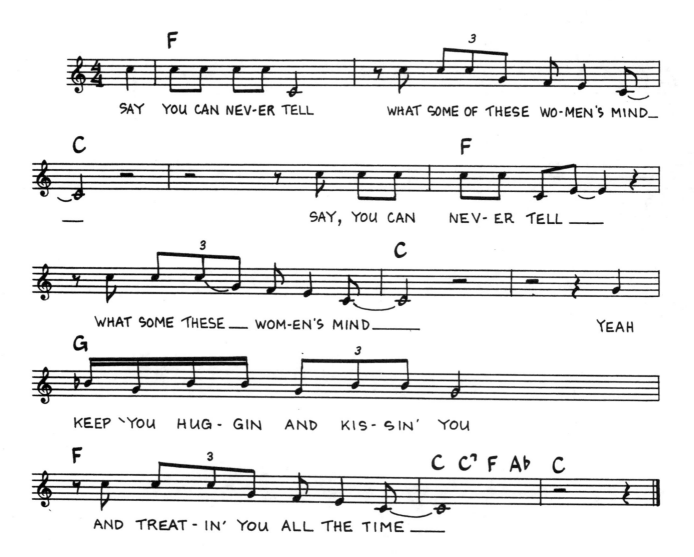

Got a gal, you call Danny Mae.
She goes out and truck all day.
She ain't crazy, she's just jivin' that way.

Skat chorus.

Have my dinner ready, don't let my coffee get cold.
Don't forget to take my sweet jellyroll.
You're not crazy, but your just jivin' that way.

Skat chorus.

She goes to bed, early at night.
Thinking about another, going to fuss and fight.
She's not crazy, she's just jivin' that way.

Skat chorus.

She goes to bed, rag tied around her head.
Thinking about another, she swears she's almost dead.
She's not crazy, she's just jivin' that way.

Skat chorus.

Hey mister, your drink run right to your head.
Had to take a bath before you went to bed.
You're no crazy but you just jivin' that way.

You Never Can Tell

By
Blind Boy Fuller

GUITAR BREAK

Lonnie Johnson

Lonnie Johnson belongs near or even at the top of great blues guitarists; his name deserves at least mention among the century's greatest non-classical guitarists. Like Blind Blake and Big Bill Broonzy, the two record stars of the 1920s who were probably his only serious instrumental rivals, Johnson is viewed primarily as a guitarist rather than a vocalist. Unlike them, he did not become a skilled musician by virtue of a ragtime background. Although Henry Townsend (who was influenced by him to take up guitar) terms Johnson "a typical blues-player", he was the one major bluesman of his generation whose work borders on jazz and who (as his accompaniments behind Louis Armstrong and Duke Ellington demonstrated) was comfortable within either format. His instrumental duets with the white jazzman Eddie Lang set a standard of musicianship that remains unsurpassed by blues guitarists. In Johnson's single string vibrato style lie the basic precedents of such jazz greats as Django Reinhardt and Charlie Christian, while B.B. King readily acknowledges Johnson's influence on his style. Thus Johnson enjoys the double distinction of having influenced musicians who themselves became enormously influential in the field of guitar-playing.

Johnson's contemporary fame and impact were practically unparalleled within the blues world itself. In addition to Townsend, he could claim numerous imitators in St. Louis, his home base of the twenties; particularly Clifford Gibson, whose tone and general flavor bear Johnson's unmistakable imprint. But Johnson's influence was not merely local or regional. His playing was closely copied by such musicians as Robert Johnson (who, as Johnnie Shines recalls, tried to palm himself off to Arkansas delta audiences as Lonnie's brother); Rambling Thomas of Logansport, Louisiana; the Alabama bluesman, Walter Roland; and Cal Smith, who played with numerous Clifford Hayes groups in Louisville, Kentucky. Today musicians like Hopson Johnson, Sonny Boy Nelson and "Guitar Pete" Franklin still play his themes. Besides flagrant imitation, his work lent itself to rear-rangement; Skip James' most brilliant instrumental piece "I'm So Glad," was undoubtedly lifted from a Johnson recording.

He was born in New Orleans, probably on February 8, 1894. As a youth, he worked in a lumber yard in addition to being part of a family ensemble headed by his father that included eleven musical sisters and a brother. Like Broonzy, he was proficient upon the violin long before taking up guitar. When his family was decimated by a wartime epidemic (probably influenza),

Johnson began his career in earnest. In 1917, he bought his first guitar; he had probably relocated in St. Louis by the time, after having visited Texas. If his travels had any influence on his guitar approach, he never spoke of it. By this time, he already had a successful career as a blues violinist, working steadily not only in New Orleans, but in a jazz band led by cornet player Charlie Creath. After a falling-out with Creath, Johnson discarded the violin and formed a trio with his brother James (Steady Roll), who played violin, and pianist DeLoise Searcy. Big Bill Broonzy, who played in St. Louis (but not with Johnson) recalled that "Lonnie was playing the violin, guitar, bass, mandolin, banjo and all the things you could make music on…"

By winning a talent contest at the Booker T. Washington Theatre in St. Louis (for 18 weeks in a row, he said), Johnson landed a recording contract. Since his first session in 1925 found him as the featured vocalist with Creath's band, it is doubtful that he had split with Creath (as his reminiscences indicated) by the time he began recording. In any event, Johnson proved an immediate success, producing an average of two titles a month during 1926.

For a time in 1927, Johnson lived in New York City, and it was probably there that he met the great Eddie Lang, who revolutionized vaudeville and jazz guitar-playing by using a flatpick. To what extent Lang's solo style, which is frequently reminiscent of Johnson's, was actually indebted to his remains an open question. Though Lang's material tended to be more sophisticated than Johnson's, Lang himself played by ear and was no more "educated" than his recording partner. Regardless, as "Bullfrog Moan" (or any of their duets) proves, their association together was one of those rare and sweet ideal combinations where the two compliment each other perfectly.

During the latter twenties, Johnson appeared on the TOBA black vaudeville circuit, a forum that was closed to nearly every other blues guitarist. His work took him to theaters from Philadelphia to Dallas, where Jesse (Babyface) Thomas, younger brother to Ramblin' Thomas, heard him play. "I thought it was the greatest thing I ever seen in my life," Thomas recalled to Dick Spottswood, "How he could play that single string melody and get a sound; his solos sounded somethin' like B.B. King, (he) makes them strings 'tremble' like that…I tried to copy some of his style." While touring in Bessie Smith's show "The Midnight Steppers" in 1929, he had a brief affair with that famous singer;

at the same time he was married to the St. Louis singer Mary Johnson. While his popularity led to lucrative professional engagements, it sometimes bore sterile fruit in hack studio sessions, resulting in unmemorable covers of "Kansas City Blues" and "Blackwater Blues." As Edith Johnson would comment to Paul Oliver: "I personally liked his blues—however they got a little monotonous after three or four years because everything was in the same tone." (He was less successful in setting his work to different keys than Blind Lemon Jefferson, but not much less so.) In his autobiography, Big Bill Broonzy would refer to Johnson's style, perhaps uncharitably, as merely "thumping a guitar." Nevertheless, when Ted Bogan arrived in Chicago from South Carolina in 1933, he heard from other musicians that Johnson was considered the city's best blues-player, an honor surely coveted by Broonzy himself.

Along with Blind Lemon and Blind Blake, Johnson was one of the first blues guitarists to achieve commercial stardom, and it was their success that greatly contributed to, if it did not in fact create, the commercial demand for country blues. By the time the Depression ended the first phase of his recording career in 1932, he had turned out over 130 sides, more than any blues singer of the period. Only forty or so sides, however, featured Johnson without some additional accompaniment, and more than half of these were recorded after 1930, when the Depression probably mandated against the use of session accompanists.

Although Johnson's earlier works continued to be issued until 1935, his live recording prospects in the mid-thirties were largely foreclosed by a dispute with Lester Melrose, the music publisher who largely ruled local recording. According to Hotbox Johnson (a disciple who moved from Louisville to St. Louis in order to learn how to play like Lonnie), Melrose refused to record him unless he changed his too-familiar guitar style. Johnson, with a display of integrity (though not of stubbornness) rare for a professional blues singer, refused to do so. The result was he enjoyed no sessions between 1932 and 1937. In person, he appeared in Chicago with the drummer Baby Dodds, and with such popular musicians as Roosevelt Sykes and John Lee (Sonny Boy) Williamson. Though his renewed recording career only ended in the early 1950s, he never quite attained his original popularity.

Johnson was working as a janitor in a Philadelphia hotel when blues enthusiast Chris Albertson persuaded him to launch a comeback in the early 1960s. His last records (using amplified guitar) bore little hint of his original greatness, and Johnson retained little enthusiasm for blues. Feeling that the music represented a racial stereotype, he preferred to play pop pieces like "Red Sails in the Sunset." Around 1966 he moved to Toronto, where he died on June 23, 1970.

In retrospect, Johnson had an unusual recording career; he had no real signature song and recorded only a few standard or traditional tunes (like "Careless Love"). Instead, he had a fund of basic arrangements that he was able to adapt to several keys: for that reason, it is often difficult to determine the keys of his non-chordal performances. On some of the works contained in this album, he may be playing in either the key of D and capoing to Eb, or playing in the key of E (his favorite) and tuning half a step low. Even within a single key or arrangement, he manages to attain so many variations in tone and accenting that his riffs are rarely predictable. He was doubly fortunate in possessing (as Big Bill and most blues guitarists did not) a superb concert guitar that was responsive to all his tonal nuances—on some sessions he probably used a Bay State model. Historically, Johnson is noted for his flat-picking approach. It is impossible that before he began recording most bluesmen only used a flatpick to play backing bass guitar. In the realm of popular entertainment, the only flatpicking guitar soloist to precede him was Nick Lucas. Yet it is said that Johnson originally fingerpicked many of his accompaniments, and was able to produce the same results.

—From the sleeve notes of *Mr. Johnson's Blues/ 1926-1932* Yazoo Records. Used with kind permission.

Stomping 'Em Along Slow

By
Lonnie Johnson

SECOND VERSE

THIRD VERSE

FOURTH VERSE

SIXTH VERSE

SEVENTH VERSE

EIGHTH VERSE

A

NINTH VERSE

TENTH VERSE

ELEVENTH VERSE

TWELFTH VERSE

THIRTEENTH VERSE

Woke Up With the Blues In My Fingers

By
Lonnie Johnson

FIFTH VERSE

Lonnie Johnson (left) with unidentified bass player.

Discography

If you are interested in pursuing the music presented in this volume, I strongly recommend the following taped guitar lesson series available from Stefan Grossman's Guitar Workshop (P.O. Box 802, Sparta, NJ 07871):

The Guitar of Rev. Gary Davis
Taught by Stefan Grossman

The Guitar of Mississippi John Hurt
Taught by Stefan Grossman

The Guitar of Lonnie Johnson
Taught by Woody Mann

The Guitar of Blind Boy Fuller
Taught by Stefan Grossman

The Guitar of Big Bill Broonzy
Taught by Woody Mann

The Guitar of Blind Blake
Taught by Woody Mann

It is essential that you hear the recordings of the four musicians presented in this collection. I would suggest the following albums (all available on compact disc and cassettes):

Mississippi John Hurt

1928 Sessions (Yazoo 1065)
Library of Congress Sessions/Avalon Blues (Flyright CD06)
Mississippi John Hurt Today! (Vanguard 79220)
The Immortal Mississippi John Hurt (Vanguard 79248)
The Best of Mississippi John Hurt (Vanguard 19/20)
Last Sessions (Vanguard 79327)

Rev. Gary Davis

Rev. Gary Davis 1936–1949 (Yazoo 1023)
Reverend Gary Davis – Ragtime Guitar & Children of Zion (Heritage CD02)
Blues and Ragtime Guitar (Shanachie Records)
Say No to the Devil (Fantasy Records)
When I Die I'll Live Again (Fantasy Records)

Blind Boy Fuller

Truckin' My Blues Away (Yazoo 1060)
Blind Boy Fuller 1930–1940 (Travelin' Man CD01)
Blind Boy Fuller – East Coast Piedmont Style (Columbia 46777)

Lonnie Johnson

Steppin' On the Blues (Columbia 46221)
Great Blues String Dazzlers (Columbia 47060)
Woke Up This Morning Blues In My Fingers (Origin Jazz Library 23)
Mr. Johnson's Blues (Yazoo Records)

Write to YAZOO RECORDS (P.O. Box 810, Newton, New Jersey 07860) for their free catalogue. They have the finest country blues reissues (on CD and cassette) available as well as a series of videos featuring Rev. Gary Davis, Son House, Mance Lipscomb, Sonny Terry, Lightning Hopkins, John Lee Hooker, Big Joe Williams, Fred McDowell, Bukka White and others. These are exciting and essential videos for your study and enjoyment of county blues.